Gauguin's Chair

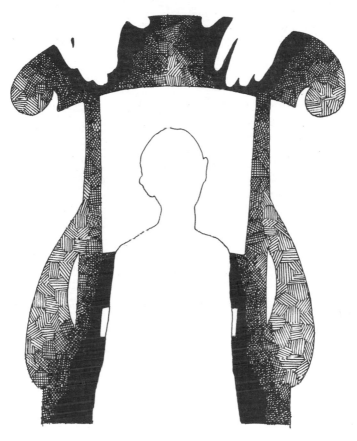

Robert Peters

Selected Poems: 1967-1974

The Crossing Press, Trumansburg, New York

ACKNOWLEDGMENTS:

We wish to thank the following publishers for permission to reprint certain poems previously published by them.

Songs for a Son, W.W. Norton, Inc., 1967.
The Sow's Head and Other Poems, Wayne State University Press, 1969.
Red Midnight Moon, Empty Elevator Shaft Press, 1973.
Cool Zebras of Light, Christopher's Books, 1974.
Connections: In the English Lake District, Anvil Press, London, 1972.

Cover—David Sykes
Photo—Max Yeh
Drawing—Harley Elliott

This project is supported by a grant from the National Endowment for the Arts in Washington, D.C., a Federal agency.

THE CROSSING PRESS SERIES OF SELECTED POETS

Library of Congress Cataloging in Publication Data

Peters, Robert Louis, 1924-
    Gauguin's chair.

    (The Crossing Press series of selected poets)
    Bibliography: p.
    I.   Title.
PS3566.E756A17   1977   811'.5'4   76-47636
ISBN O-912278-73-O
ISBN 0-912278-74-9 pbk.

Gauguin's Chair

For Jeff, May, Rob
and for Paul

Contents

Shall you uncover honey/where maggots are?

-- Charles Olson

ONE:
Wisconsin

EAGLE RIVER, WISCONSIN

Gangsters
came to Eagle River
but not one singer
writer or painter.

I can show you
where Dillinger sweated
at little Bohemia

where Mayor Kelly
rubbed his belly
and shot
well bodyguarded
rounds of golf

where Capone's crew
sniffed danger
adjusted their nickers
masqueraded as berrypickers
in the less ominous
air of Eagle River
when the home zoo
grew too hot

and governors
La Follette and Heil
paused awhile
patted their wallets
observed the state
of the wild blueberry crop

gathered votes
were startled to note
so few folk
in that beautiful
backwoods of
logged off, mined-out
land. And Herbert Hoover
chose the Brule
for hooking his trout
saw Eagle River
as nothing to shout about.

And yet
one could/can
flounder
up to his eyes
there, and the mind could/can
blunder
frenzied there,
poems choking the throat.

FATHER

He would enter
the enfolding woods
slip into shadow
velvet
and return late
often with game
materialize
hours after
I had seen him
transformed into
treebranch, into wolf
crushed by storm
or tree
bloodsmear on
snowcrust

Or with his brains blown out
by accident
or design:
well-distributed shell
the brain embossed. . .

But he always returned
silence his evidence
for the ephemeral whispers
immensities
garnered from the
blood cells of swamps
the ventricles of trees
the cavities of his own heart,
from a flashlight cell.

THE BUTCHERING: Eagle River, Wisconsin

I

Dad told me to hold the knife,
and the pan. I heard the click
on wood of the bullet inserted,
rammed. Saw a flicker thrash
in a tree beside the trough,
saw a grain in the sow's mouth,
felt my guts slosh.

"Stand back," dad said.
Waffled snowtrack
pressed by his boots and mine.
Blood and foam. "Keep the knife
sharp, son, and hold the pan."
One of us had shuffled,
tramped a design,
feet near the jackpine.
"She'll bleed slow.
Catch all the blood you can."

A rose unfolded, froze.
"Can't we wait?" I said.
"It should turn warmer."

Spark, spark buzzing
in the dark.

"It's time," dad said, and
waited.

II

Bless all this beauty! preacher
had exclaimed; *all sin and beauty
in this world! Beast and innocent!*

Fistbones gripped the foreshortened
pulpit rim. Thick glasses drove
his furious pupils in.

III

Dad brought the rifle to the skull.
The sow's nose plunged into the swill,
the tips of her white tallow ears as well.
Splunk! Straight through the brain, suet
and shell. Stunned! Discharge of food,
bran. Twitch of an ear. Potato, carrot,
turnip slab. "Quick. The knife, the pan."

He sliced the throat.
The eye closed over.
Hairy ears stood up, collapsed.
Her blood soured into gelatin.
She had begun to shit.

IV

We dragged her
to the block and tackle rig.
We tied her tendons, raised her,
sloshed her up and down.
We shaved her hair,
spun her around, cut off
her feet and knuckles,
hacked off her head,
slashed her belly
from asshole down through
bleached fat throat.
Jewels spilled out
crotches of arteries
fluids danced and ran.

We hoisted her
out of dog reach
dumped her entrails
in the snow
left the head
for the dogs to eat--
my mother disliked headmeat.
The liver, steaming, monochrome,
quivered with eyes.
We took it home.

V

I went to my room.
Tongues licked my neck.
I spread my arms,
threw back my head.
The tendons of a heel
snapped.
What had I lost?
bit   bridle   rage?

Preacher in his pulpit
fiddling, vestments aflame.
He, blazing, stepping down
to me. Hot piss came.
I knelt on the floor,
bent over, head in arms.
Piss washed down, more.
I clasped my loins, choked
cock, scrotum. Arm crossed
over arm. And I cried
(dry marble) loving my guts,
O vulnerable guts,
guts of creatures.

MOTHER

Woman
straining over a washtub
in an iceshed
of a house
chinked with moss
veiled with tarpaper

house alive with mice
in warm weather,
in cold with ice.

Your stuttering washlines
strung up
through the house:
slab underwear (flat
salted fillets) sheets,
shirts, board-stiff
dresses, nightshirts.

And pancakes
whipped out of batter
kept in a crock
fermenting on the back
of the woodstove.

And peanutbutter (county relief)
extended by blendings
of bacon drippings. . .

Strip away all subsequent
events! Repeat those
gestures! Goad us

out to the pasture,
to the starved potato field
and the bean field
while you prod, curse
your life, the vagaries
of dreams. . .

A beast
crouches near--
fur of cedar and ash,
willowbranch for claws--
toothscraps from a
glacierbone--licks
with hot tongue
the barn, the loghouse.
Licks at
patch of sandground

kept clear for crops
for sow, calf, and hens
breathing, freezing

as night (a peddlar)
drops
a poisoned seed,
and a
wreathing fog
settles in
    soft underbelly
    soft thighs
tight against the throat
dark lovely throat
of night. I crouch again
waiting, hoping you are near.

THE SOW'S HEAD

The day was like pewter.
The gray lake a coat
open at the throat. The border
of trees--frayed mantle collar,
hairs, evergreen. The sky dun.
Chilling breeze. Hem of winter.

I passed the iodine-colored brook
hard waters open
the weight of the sow's head
an ache from shoulder to waist,
the crook of my elbow numb;
juices seeping through
the wrapping paper.

I was wrong to take it.
There were meals in it.
I would, dad said, assist
with slaughter, scrape off
hair, gather blood.
I would be whipped for
thieving from the dogs.

I crossed ice
which shivered, shone.
No heads below, none;
nor groans--only water, deep,
and the mud beds of frogs asleep;
not a bush quivered,
not a stone. Snow.

Old snow had formed
hard swirls   bone
and planes with
windwhipped ridges
for walking upon;
and beneath, in the deep,
bass quiet, perch whirling
fins, bluegills, sunfish,
dim-eyed, soaking heat.
Mud would be soft down there,
rich, tan, deeper than a man:
silt of leeches, leaves
tumbling in from trees,
loon feces, mulch-thick,
mudquick, and lignite forming,
cells rumbling, rifts.

I knelt, chopped through
layers of ice until
water, pus, spilled up
choking the wound. I widened
the gash. Tchick! Tchick!
Chips of ice flew.
Water blew from the hole,
the well, a whale, expired.
My knees were stuck to the ice.

I unwrapped the paper.
The head appeared
shorn of its beard,

its ears stood up, the snout
with its tinkertoy holes
held blood, its eyes were shut,
there was grain on its mouth.

It sat on the snow
as though it lived below,
leviathan come for air
limbs and hulk
dumb to my presence there.

I raised the sow's head
by its ears. I held it
over the hole, let it go,
watched it sink, a glimmer
of pink, a wink of a match
an eyelid. . .

A bone in my side beat.

FEW OF US FEEL SAFE ANYWHERE

I recall
digging up moleroutes,
looking for moles,
in a primitive schoolyard
in northern Wisconsin.
The mangy grass
bound and flattened by
mud and water rose up
beneath soft channels
burrowed by molesnouts.

I unearthed
a fertile nest, fought
down two friends to keep
the blind pink furless
creatures to myself,
warm between my hands.

I won by
running up to teacher,
intending to present her
with those jewels, my catch
a quest, possession all
my own, for her, my lover.

But others
watched, grinned
as I drew apart those palms,
revealed those pinkish forms,
stilled, calm, their shanks
of legs drawn up beneath
their toothless jaws, their
whiskers bent, their mouths
each bearing blood.

WHAT JOHN DILLINGER MEANT TO ME

The Wisconsin lodge
that Dillinger shot up
where he slept with
Evelyn Frechette
in a musty bedroom
hung with staghorns
is legend, has become
locale.

> *Last week there were*
> *arbutus, this week violets,*
> *and next there will be snow.*

Here was Robin Hood,
thirsting, despising law,
loner, who by miracle
knew and fled,
left Evelyn behind,
her and her friend.

> *And snow follows snow.*
> *Flickers peck the trunks*
> *of evergreens seeking*
> *grubs and nuts*
> *stored there by squirrels.*

> *Bears lie fallow,*
> *the paps of summer*
> *in their dreams. Skunks*
> *garner oil, rub their*
> *legs together to*
> *quiet the seeping.*

I did not see the pustules
on his jaw, the chipped tooth,

the crooked finger, the fact
that he had clap. His hands
were beautiful. His breath
as fragrant as one of
Solomon's lovers.

And his picture
on my bedroom wall,
pasted to the corrugated box
smashed flat and nailed
to the two-by-fours to
keep out cold! How immaculate
his stance before his flivver!
Felt hat back
on his head, shirt sleeves
rolled above the elbow,
trousers high on the waist,
a band, Hollywood style,
set with pearls to hold them
tight. His legs spread wide,
and, held even with his navel,
his tommy gun. Again
the stance, a perfect V,
zodiac man.

What had gone wrong
at the forked bridge
outside the town? What
had transpired at
Sunday School? Was it
poverty? Despair?
The wheel at the fair?

The gingerbread man
rides the stream
on the slick nose of the fox,
Robin Hood romps in a costume,
Arthur in armor.

TWELVE

At twelve
I had myself baptized
induced my family to attend church
taught sunday school
mowed down various
adolescent heresies
with the jawbone of my
zeal, sang Solomon's songs
and erotic hymns
savored the cannibalism
of wafer and wine, made
the saviour's wounds my own
displayed myself upon crosses
prayed myself into onanistic
sweats during pounding
thunderstorms, dressed in a
sheet, communed with my
lover, saw the world
entirely as glass.

LUCY ROBINSON

Lucy Robinson's
rimless spectacles
rode athwart her nose.
About her neck
were chunks of fur
which made it appear
that she had tiny rabbits on.
Masses of hair
hung down her face
(old curtains belted low
about the waist). Her
wrists were fat. Her
hands were knobs, the
knuckles bumps and knots
which creaked to open.
Her mouth seldom parted
when she spoke.

Through the musty curtains
she would come
shattering the sleep
of moths, hums of flies,
raising dust.

Massive creature!
keeping the shoestore
in the parlor
of her decayed lath house,
selling one pair a day,
two before school began
and more for Santa Claus.

I see her with a box
fetched from a shelf
behind a cage. Dad
pulls me up, points
to a brightening shoe.

Lucy wheezes and the light
is dim. Her arthritic
finger latches in
behind my heel. A dead bird.
I feel its bill.

I want her hand free!
the size to be right!
The shoes will pinch and blister.
I shall have to break them in evenings
drawing water for the cows!

She stuffs dollars
into the tight mouse
of her hand, whiskers
on her knuckles twitch,
and whiskers on her mouth. . .

In that debris,
in the dust
a hunger now--except for
an image, a lampwink,
a jewel, a gland
(faint radium pulse)
a spotted lung, striations
on a hand, an arthritic spur,
a claw quivering near a baseboard
hole. . .what have you done
Lucy Robinson.

SEVENTEEN

1

Meet me
in the dark
root cellar

earth, a kerosene
light, burlap,
no thought of morning

to answer this
why without
flowers you

overwhelm me
with orchids
and violets

to the act of
my loving you
myself as
rigid earth in
the darkness
lying

without blankets
for hours
in the musk

without caring
brought into it
into its particular

treasure, the
pounding hooves
of goats, the
red tongues of
parrots.

2

It was
a mood
disrupting
the black fog
throwing off
singly
the burlap bags

Who could be
natural?

the pickle jars
sneering overhead
the stench of
rotting potatoes
whiffed sensuality
fat wet mushrooms,
carrots, onions
softening.

Nor did
fantasy work.
erect it shrivelled
when you said
"don't be dirty."

I dropped free
dressed again
in the black house
of my own
clothing
but did not know it.

CANOE JOURNEY

I

I pass demolished trees
where a storm
has splattered them.
Debris is kindlingspun.

I slide beneath
tamarack and spruce.

The dipping of a spoon
into a springful of water.

Grabbing branches
I slide the boat along
pass through
bronchial tangle, heart
system.

The air is sweet
with alcohol and blood,
no houses near
no farms
deserted

A spray of water,
a branch of hemlock
strikes my face.

I skim through
what I have been.

I come to a meadow
faint frozen green
red moss-spoors
the sky smokey
anger in the clouds,
blue, a dram of it, and red/

The blue vanishes.
The sun faint,
hurricanic.

I beach the canoe.
Birds rise.
The canoe wavers
at sapling anchor
strains for midstream
and lake, muskellenge
in cold waterbrake.

And beneath my feet
beneath the marshgrass
routes for ferrets
tracks for snouts, mouths
feeding on veins,
capillary streams.

My boots are soaked
past the laces.

I am in past my knees.

II

Pikeweed
trails from my hand.
Canoe drags
greenroots after
mesh of water   fisherman

on cobblestone
on world, rattle of throat, of
petrifying heart.
Weeds clamor in the dark.

A mouth
gelatin hard
breaks the surface.

A muskellenge strikes,
swirls and sinks. Water
and a stone
mica-shining below.

Legs braced towards prow
and keel.
I crave for a voice, for
a hunter (my father), for
a soldier, for Rimbaud,
a swimmer....

III

Whish and slash
of weedspear
scrape and tear of
lilypad and branches.

The prow rises.
Paddle drips
fine silt.

Air, sharp diamond
pricks my throat.
My shirt is soaked.

IV

Shiver of breeze.
Open water achieved.

I rock
in a brainful of weeds
arms crossed over
bent forward.
I see
the north sky
slide with icelight
in daylight.

A wind clatters,
shakes reeds and grasses
drenched
with ice.

Fishfins
encased in water
wink.

The canoe fans, turns
upon a vitrescible wave
the color of cinnamon.

The sun blisters forth
lung-scarlet

as the reedbeds begin again
before the ashcolored trees
rise and firtrees bleed
green. A tangle within
a body, within a breast, a
heart.

A merganser honks, banks
drops a shadow
strikes to the north
disappears.
A claw draws up a black lamp
towards Cassiopeia.

TWO:
Richard

MOTIF

I

These are fragments
of pain, stalactites
of the heart doomed
to melt, leveling panic
the jab in the guts
the slick vein leaping
over my hand
perplexed sick
over its branchings
multiform.

II

In winter
a bird drops
from a bough;
the snow entombs him
wraps him in.

When spring
unlocks the forest
feathers stiffen
wings collapse
pinoil grease
thaws and dries
beak whitens
eyejuice melts
internally
flesh softens
a purple stain.

THEME

I call your name, son,
festooned and touched
with amber in my mind:
Richard.   Peace.

The apple turns to ash,
the slumbering worm
begins to swell, stir,
prepares his rubbery mouth
for the assault.

I run a cinder
through my palm,
firing the ember

and my flesh
burns as
heart drains
its fear--
flick of a
worm's beak.

The sun comes down.
It stamps its lamp
against my brain.
I shielded, shield my eyes
against the glare!   Where
are you gone, son?
Where?   Where?

REPORT

I turned you, Richard,
kissed your neck
to wake you
from that fever-breaking sleep
and saw
your blue cracked lip
the stark death-mark.

HOSPITAL

Wheeze away, O green steel tank!
Breathe, gray nosecup set
over the hardening cartilage
of his nose!

>(Unsheeted form
>on a wheeled-in table;
>robe, fresh urinestain
>on the pajamas--designs
>of tugboats, bedroom
>slippers.)

Mechanical sustainer! Push those lungs,
inflate them, swell them! Shock them
into breath again!

>(Brut heads
>hands probing
>detecting
>over the
>wheeled-in table).

O neutral doctor! O delicate finger
laboring! O pluck the heart (fat
and vein) blood-fretted jewel; strum
melody

>He does not breathe!)

dredge out the heart and
shake it, slap it, bathe it
in the glare of the
stainless light
above the wheeled-in table;
massage it   prick it
be brutal, hand, be god
prick the quiescent
                    immobile
                        gem

TRANSFORMATION

Between death's
hot coppery sides
the slime of birth
becomes a chalky
track of bone
compressed in time
to slate, or gneiss,
or marble--pressed
lifeless into stone.

They will never remember
one so young, or one so
mirthful, or one so
quiet in his bed.

DANCE

A brain danced in the wind
A natural shape for a natural
mind--its motions diaphanous.
Outrageous performer!

    no rod, stick, string,
    or invisible hand.

Clouds rose behind it.

Music I could not hear
(but only imagined)
whirled into sound:
tunes for an oboe
tambourine and violin.
A brain danced in the wind.

There were no trees at hand.
Birds settled to earth
and slept on warm stones
wing-fast. A brain
danced in the wind.

FEVER

We did not seek
this monument, nor
ever wished it:
bed, drawn shade,
steamer vaporing
the room, peeling
the sill, smoking
the lungs (slender
ferny tracks
born of an ancient sea),
and fever, loathsome
traveler with his
pack all rolled,
his blanket ready
for the tryst, a
true fire, reedy,
igniting, his
destination
our son's dear
capital, his
helpless brain!

KITTENS

The kittens came tonight,
the ones you'd wished for
when you broke
the hen's breast-bone
that Wednesday, death-day
morning. You had asked for
plump dark woolly cats
with eyes like olives,
glossy; cats tumbling
on the floor soundless,
pricking at string,
lapping up blue milk,
their abdomens
as tight as udders.

This was the scene:
the brindled cat squirmed
beneath the chair,
whined, rose, and
plunged, spread-legged
through the room
to find a box, a hat,
a place by a commode
for birth. We set
a blue crate for her,
spread down a towel
and waited. Two
shaky forms appeared
smeared with blood,
fur wet like licorice,
eyelids swollen.
The mother screamed
(an angry rip of cloth),
glanced swiftly back,

impelled by burning muscle
found the wet cowering lumps,
peeled then swallowed
their rubbery translucent
coats, lent her tongue
to smear the wobbling
panting forms all shiny
bound with feebleness;
ink-black they fell
into a land of honey:
then dropped the third
and last.

But earlier, on wish-day
death-day, poised
on my mound of sand,
I'd said "No cats,"
and quelled your joy
with news of chance
loose from the zoo
against you: "No
mice, no toads, no turtles,
salamanders, frogs"--
I made a catalogue--
"they die.
Their little toes
curl up like leaves,
their waxy eyes go shut,
their tails hang limp
their whiskers droop."

Dreading each death's
advent, I sought to
spare you.   Each lost
pet might break deep,
deep within your heart,
might crystallize its

red wet velvet sides
into long beads of rice
to feed the worm--
or snap them into
tears like seeds
to break on stone:
each death a buzz, an
eel's tail slapped
against your knee,
a blue, a fatal jolt!

In proof I said,
"Count up your pets:
the molting snake
gashed half-way to
its tail, remember
him?" We speared Snake
food (some, living,
bled on toothpicks)
and thrust them past
the forked and flicking
palate, the svelte
unhinging jaws.
But Snake died
rolled like an earthworm
in his leaves.

Then Mouse: remember
how you bore him
through the yard
wrapped in his hard
leaf-shroud, his green tail
sprinkling mortality
like ivy-juice
all over you that day?
You brought a metal pail,
spilled water in the hole

torn by your rusted shovel.
You wept and gracefully
placed Mouse beneath a
tulip root. Two nails
formed a cross, a fallen
leaf the saviour. There
Mouse still lies set
by your own hands
firmly into place--
unless the earth with
acid formed from oaks
has decomposed his bones,
like yours, to ash,
and slipped all down
between packed grains
of quartzite, sandstone,
beryl, smoothed out with
lime and all the other
flavors of an earthy crypt.

But all my scare
of zoo and deep-felled
nightmare failed
and would not settle
in your brain's mailed
small hole for fear,
where clung invisible
the hung smoke of the
sleeping fatal fever.
I smiled broadly from
the table, hitched up
my belt, enjoyed your
able innocence, bade you
break the bone and gladly
eat your wish.

With shy delight you
seized the dish, took up
and sprung the wing, turned

it like stone to see through
in the light, sprung it wide,
asked it to snap, to softly
free your wish:

      jarring the light-hung
      particles of dust
      caught near the window
      the bone did break!

Our house now
crawls with kittens.
They tumble, stumble, run,
find bits of sun,
find mother's udders,
mews. They lick themselves
waver on unfirm claws,
do all the acts,
make all the gestures that
you knew live kittens make.

I'm glad you took
these facts with you
into the night! I'd
rather have you take
these kitten facts along
than all the history
you never came to know,
the shouts of passion,
war; the violence of cars;
the poetry that never
broke itself against
your ears. O
that there had been more!

MEMORY

I wait, I lift the
corner of the tape
and spy a wound
as pale as lung
burnished
with alcohol, the
red petals of a
scar, a wet eye,
winking, winking.

I sing for you Richard
and for your coatbutton
loose, the untied shoes,
the collar open at the throat,
nor would the bathrobe close,
the chord was gone,
the nurse had failed
to see. . .

WOUND

The wound is closing in:
flakes, gold horny substance,
salmon ridge, miniscule
orange craters
bearing red centers.

I unlatch
the surgeon's clips,
grind glass between flat stones,
impale a splinter
under my nail,
lift the
hardened corners
of the wound, tear
flesh into strips,

endure nausea,
whorls of hurt,
and free the gelatin,
the cells, the salmon ridge,
and drop in
glass, sand,
bits of chaff,
press,
release fresh blood,
watch it spurt.

WALL

Let's wait beside
the nonsense wall,
all dread: white flaking
bricks, dust for tears,
for scissors, paste.

"Spratt and wife," I say
to call you back. "Cow,
dog, moon, and spoon," I
try again. The air
flows hollow. "Burst, fat,
hungering George who flew
away, was never seen." I
laugh, assume a troll's voice:
"The Human Pole, a string
of a man with all his
buttons lost, nibbling
a fat brown roll; Tucker
wanting supper, the stolen
tarts, the jack of hearts
snapped flat against the
deck, breaded honey, black-
bird, the nurse's blear
proboscis stuck to an icy
line, Riding Hood's basket
adorned with silk, with milk,
the wolf's meal, the squeal,
and grandma freed--grotesque
and happy birth!"

PRESERVE

I see that mass of trees:
moist veins
racked against the sky
mortal backdrop
for a world of
twig, black leaf, and
large hill riddled
with mange and rot;

and beneath your feet
a bridge, snowy,
with crisp flakes
spun from the hooves
of does in troll-land
frightened for their young.

There, dazzled by
blue light, by ice,
you sped through the
morning: your boot
buckles clicking and
red mittens pointing
(hands on film)
toward each frozen
wonder of the trail:

globes of cowfat
tied in mesh and
stuck with seeds
(corn, oat, sunflower,
rice) swung from branches;
coconut skulls
filled with meal,
fists of oak, wood-knobs
smeared with grease,
and rinds of orange,
and powdered milk

in bottles, to feed
the birds.

Birds shivered
as we passed.
And on you ran.

I called out to you,
called out to you, boy,
saw your prints and joy
skim through the water
spin like the bugs
we saw in summer
on the drugged lake,
flung pebbles at,
begged time to flounder.

On you sped
through woods and brush
passed the pike-weed
marsh, the beaver dam.

I caught your sparkle
toward the rounding bay
drenched with sun
fisherman.

"Keep, keep within sight
of land,"   I cried;
"of every riddle, joy,
the pains of Christmas,
Easter, grandma's house,
the fair"--the prompting
died.

"The enemy!" you screamed,
and with your sister
leaped the brook
a month before the close,
before
        the trap sprang
before
        the ice rang in
        and froze your
        mouth, heart
        glorious eyes and limbs:
        ice-flowers of death,
        blue, exfoliate utterly!

EASTER

Meredith gave up her doll
last night. You would not
have known his face, so
aged it was. Soap was
hopeless. His rag cheeks
were cancerous. His lips,
still smiling, mocked
decay. Raggedy-Andy,
Raggedy Andy. Meredith
wrote a note: "Spirit
him off to Easterland."
She kissed him. "One
more day to live," she
said. "One night to live."
She left him in his chair.
By morning
he was gone.

Play with him, Richard.
She asks it.
Keep his gray face.
Kiss all death
from his buttoned eyes.
Kiss sleep from his mouth.

SONG FOR A SON

My son's image
was painted on sand.

The wind from off the lake
bears me no news of him,
nor of his impression.

Was it arrogance to think
I could hold his features?

I had set them in memory,
fashioned cameos for the
mind, had seen that face at will,
in various attitudes, transforming
me--when he was alive.

But I am blind!
Unable to create a brow,
a lash, the hollow down
the back of the neck,
the throat!

Look.
Those trees hold nothing
in their branches. Those rushes
by the lake, so rife with
blackbirds, hold nothing:

     Mist faces,
     faces in shrouds,
     faces in clouds. . .
Water has worn the cameos down

ENCOUNTER

You heard, son,
the ominous
beat-skip-beat
of the heart

and scrambled down
from the yellow swing
bearing mouse in hand

and saw the red trickle,
the straightened tail,
the eye glazed pink,
the paws curled in.

OH, CABIN MICE!

Frenzied by the smell
of stale bread, jam,
and meat locked up
for the season, cabin mice
in the dead of winter
scamper over carpets,
up and down cupboards,
beat paths around the
fireplace, discover
envelopes of grain
poisoned pellets
prepared for them.

They ignore
tails and whiskers,
female heat, lice
in their fur, the
puddle of snow-water
under the door,
decree sharp teeth,
squeal, squirm, nip,
and draw mouseblood,
leap over each other,
sate themselves,
grow tranquil at last,
serene, tummied (the
tits of the mother mice
bursting with fresh-
pastured milk from
the granary), make
lingering copulations

just before
the advent of
slow blood
deterioration
of cell walls

hemophilia
falsely induced
swelling up
of hot breath
charred lungs, blood
seeping

and the trip
outside, into the cold,
away from the
suffocating cabin eaves.

And a bright aster
forms at the mouth,
snowbloom, leaves
blooming in the snow,
and a bright calendula
unfolds
    beneath the tail.

SNOW

I shall never touch snow
and not see your plaid coat
and the blue cap
with flaps like
small rabbits
by your ears.

TURTLES AND MICE

As we grope, son,
seek you again,
your coat, laces,
rusting skates, and
black stuffed seal
hugged beneath
your stiffening arm,
and seek you
in your squiggles
made on paper,
the turtles you cut out,
bent the legs of
so they'd walk,
and placed them
on a farm with mice,
blind, a troll waits,
his spiked head
turned toward
the west
his eye a sapphire
in the dusk.

TROLL

Never tell that tale,
bright child.   Never say
the fantasies, for they do
come true.   They transpire
on mild mornings when the
pale spindly woods mourn
for the sap locked
in their roots.

I am your troll, bright child tramping
on the bridge: for who
has seen the wind?
and who
among the leaves
hangs trembling?

THE BURIAL OF THE ASHES

I

I take you from the church
in a brown leathery
cube. I cannot read
the label, the facts
of ash. A car, passing,
throws sun against
my face--a clarion.

I ask for a shovel.
"No trouble," says the
preacher. I follow,
pass through
Gethsemane.

We have trouble
with the shovel:
gone from its place--
a plain fact askew.

I fear that the winds
will howl soundless
again.

We find a spade,
though not the one
we wished; and I
lead the way
to a bush on a
rolling slope
set with rock
like the fringe
of a well.
The crown of the
green bush wavers.

I open the box:
a sack, translucent,
crammed with scraps
of brown black white
and yellow bone.

60

I test the weight,
press the sack to my
cheek, hold it
to my eyes.

Sun streams through,
turns that ivory to
gold, that pale pale
white to blue, those bits
of brown to red!

II

I break the earth
(the spade moves well).
I prune a root
and smooth the hole.
I press the earth
by hand, drop in
a leaf and kneel.
I crumble-in loam.
As grains slip through
I hunger to count them,
I hunger to count them.

I hope for silence,
vision, a shimmering
saint bearing a twig
studded with emeralds,
a gift.

Richard, Richard,
there was snow that day
and sun enough
to dazzle empires
when you ran laughing
beside the frosty lake,
mortal, lovely, mine.

CODA

I

Stars burst,
pin back the sable
for a glance, then fade.

Petals drop from the vine
and the pink grape blackens,
the fig contains the worm,
leaves yellow and drop

rust swallows the metal
frames supporting.

Beside the lake the beaver
slap their tails.   In the
deep lake fish glimmer.

On the water wild geese
wait.   Tomorrow their
keen breasts shall beat
streams of stars.

You loved it here!

II

Our thrusts
are scarcely marble.
They crumble.   (There is
no private art.   We write
what we can).   Our leapings
fade.   So does our burbling
mirth.   Our begging and
begetting, they too pass
over the fury of the hour.

What we seek, what binds us,
is a wish to share with
sleek beasts waiting
in the fields, all turned
head to head, toward the
waning sun, a semblance
of calm.

Richard Nathaniel Frank Peters:
Sept. 18, 1955-Feb. 10, 1960

THREE:
Wolfmilk

ARROGANCE

In the end
a man
loves himself
alone.

The elements, and the stars
though stronger and more beautiful
than he, rest, blow, quench, burn
and glow for him alone--he thinks.

Strangers, tribes and crowds
he frowns upon, transcends.
The lucency of God floods over
them and him, illuminates his wit,
shines dimly by comparison
on theirs.   Out of His tolerance
God *lets* them be.

His relatives one by one
he drops; and learning
he ignores, and art (for
insight twists his heart).
He shrinks, like lead
boiling down.   "I shape
the universe!" he cries.
Scales over his eyes
remove all doubt.

In the end
it is only himself
he sees
loves
    thinks about.

IN THE FOREST: Rock-Figure
in a Stream

Water leaps
from the pool's hands
spills over logs and boulders.
There are children in the forest.

A cinder-colored rock
shaped like a man's head
submerged to the chin:
his mouth rides clear
chin sucks water in
swirling around it
pinched nose
eyes inset over the ridge
of the nose, left eye
suspended, forehead,
a gouge.

Eddies swirl
past a nut-strewn
hemlock bough
out of lip-reach.

I am with him.   I taste
the nuts.   A needle
cuts my eye.   I thirst.
Scarlet grips my tongue.
I spit lung substance--
hemlock kernels cracked
and broken--spit this
onto stone where rain
will wash it down
into the mouth   slaking hunger
intensifying thirst.

FOR EMANUEL SWEDENBORG

A temple, you said,
or body muscle--
soldiers arrayed
efflorescences
put out by
hosts of artillery
on parade

Aaron's breastplate glitters
David's sling is blazing

Our palette
violent in its hues
lacks molten metal
lights but keeps
your darks

Perhaps we shall
discern, perhaps
we won't
           Meanwhile
rock, hill and
galled shoulder--facts
boil over, strike us
on the mouth. So late,
so late. As deserters
murphymen from the
phalanx you envisioned
approach seeking
flesh, cash, a fix.

WINE BEARER

As you
fetch the bottle
from the cellar

down there
dandelion blossoms
steeped in darkness
pink vaginal
mushrooms
girl creatures

Your head first
the blue shirt
all of a swing
and a haste
uncorking
and a shimmer

Place it here
earthmold
stained green
glass bottle

as you ascend
from the
rootcellar
running
to the river

CONISTON WATER: In Memory of the English Speed-Boat Racer Donald Campbell

I

I thought I had caught
a piece of Donald Campbell's
jaw in Coniston Water.

The lake, calm,
seemed firm enough
for walking upon,
weighted and still.
Skeletal fingers
in the silt
had drawn the surface
water taut.

But on retrieving it
with a stick
I saw that it was
part of a ram.

Touched with bracken
mountains rise like
camels about to be broken
over Coniston Water.

The rain is icy,
shoots channels
forming streams and
wild falls.   The lake
is cinders fallen.

I imagined the spray
as *Bluebird III*
burst aloft that
January day, jet engine

propelling her away
300 miles per hour
dropped
            over the lake.

And I saw his kodakpicture
('34), standing with his father
facing Windermere,
fantastic speed dream
already there
irritating the gum line
of a forward tooth.
Career. Father to blonde son.
Record to be broken.
Son to father.

II

Now,
citizens declare
that divers found
his helmet with his head
intact--but nothing else.
British newsmen joke, "Can
the water, Campbell Soup."
The search goes on,
transpires in smoke.
The press is dumb
silent on skull
jawbone, femur, thumb.

Stunned
by the rocketing, fish
quiver (the lake is deep);
their throats brush leaves
decaying turning
infinitesimally
to mulch; fish hover,
may never ascend
again, may never spawn.

That morning
when his helmet clicked
shut he knew, they say,
that he had struck
on the fatal hour (fine
trial run), felt
in his spine the earlier
chill of hearing that his
father was dead, in his
own boat.

Is daring suicide?
Is it degree that matters
swaggering before
the skeletons of others
pushing
while doing the same?
To live is to stand
with ankles bare
and tendons bare.

The skull guards the brain,
the ribcage the lungs
and wheezing heart.

Enter a street, drop
hand to lake water,
cast a stone, collect
the mail, lift fork
or knife to mouth,
press tongue to
incisor--rehearse for
suicide! A diamond
has its price, its fire.
A witch squeezes a toad
to her dug, begs it
suck--as dogs chew
on one another, calves
gouge other calves
with horns, and women
naturally abuse their children.

The fact
        of wanting to live
assumes
        a desire to die.

O, Campbell,
drifting, wavering

where there are no
plants, lice, scum,
where tinted scraps of
bluebird shake, grate
soundless, roll, turn and
roll. . .
        wait
                wait.

CHRISTMAS POEM 1966

Lines on an English Butcher-Shop Window

O beautiful severed head of hog
O skewered lamb-throat, marble eye of
   duck, O meadow-freshened hare
      suspended
O lovely unplucked pheasant
   ripening in the gloom
O gracious suckling pig upended
O twisted tail erect
   and pinkish gouged-out hole
O graceful nub of sow tit, merry xylophone
   of fractured ribs
O rib ends smarting where the saw
   has severed you
O pleasant rind of fat and rosy spume
   along the incision sliced
      from genitals to snout
O livers tumbling, O clattering
   jewel of pancreas and
      ligaments of stomach wall
O golden brains emplattered
O calf-groin hacked in two
O carcass spiked, with legs
   encasedand tied about
      with paper, hanging on the wall
O sheep form, severed shoulders,
O ham string of ox, O whitening lyre,
O steer loin pierced, O haunch,
O ribcage disembowelled
O glorious trays and juices, heaps of
   lambhearts, chicken livers,
      gizzards, claws
I see you all!

PREMONITION

I'll return again
said the face.
Oh no
replied the ear
and turned aside.
A finger
stood erect, a shadow
rabbit's ear garnering
messages from the wind.
The hand's palm was
red and wet.

There is pulp
on the sidewalk.
By the water-
fountain bird
bath in the garden
a wren's heart
is impaled
on a thorn.
Love is
gentler than sight--
that is its burden.

BLUE BOY

Trees
seem to
follow you

Worms bleed
on the sidewalk
out of morning
crushed into
fat thumbends pulp

I descend

Noise rages
over the fire

They are closing
the canyon again

smothering out
the word--that we
lean towards
each other
sway

All this
as I follow
as your arms swing
scatter water-reflections
of charged rock:
the design of a
pomegranate split open

What ruin shoots
towards you walking,
strikes my skull,
pits sword to skullbone,
spears down
the gristle of the
spinal track?

Observe the dogs
hung up   rod to anus
anus to rod
beneath the
magnolia tree

we slip into morning
into afternoon.

SO FAR, FEW WOLF CHILDREN
HAVE BEEN AUTHENTICATED

I walk all night, craving.
adorned white horses
prance, jingle
bridlebells, raise
hooves, eyes
sapphirebright.

What to do
when lust
swallows its own
breath, waits
frog-gutted, tummied,
to feel a straw
shoved up its ass
threatens to burst,
unless additional
pressure is produced.

If my hair were gray
and longer
if my will were
stronger and I
had no debts. . .

it is the wolf,
keen moonhowler,
that we seek,
and a stance
in a field of stones,
and rain, drizzling

sleet   hail
and at last a cave
of guano, fragrant
the debris coughed up
by owls (sweet small
deer devoured), a
nest of leaves,
and a shewolf braced
on all fours, pumice-toned
udder exposed, nipples
erect, at right angles,
to be sucked gummed
by desperate ones.

Dreams
fall out of the nest
of chaste moments.
Slate-colored proprieties
at last
        drown
            as the mouth
dribbles, runs
with fresh white wolfmilk.

ON SECURING A FRIEND'S SLIPPED
CONTACT LENS

Night comes on
we halt
on the walk
beside the lamp
before the lighted shop

The sun has dropped
you cannot see

I lift the eyelid
scan for the lens
locate it
where fine hair
begins
        wonder
how to move it
to its place
without impacting
grain   soot   scratch
of diamond on
gelatinous glass.

Glass moves
rising, adhering now

I touch eye-water.

Night comes on
it is the skin
that fails to
let us in.

FEN BULLS NEAR CAMBRIDGE

Samuel Palmer, you said
they say he never saw
what he painted, out there

dusk, landscape floundering
crumbling sod
crumbling in fingers,
shredded ancient skeletons
and bones.

The grainfield
   chokes his trees
rises upon
   a middle tier
of branches

His elms are flogged
up to their crotches
by grass
   their rolling shapes
succumb
   to the field.

His arrangement:
   the red sun
   over the fen
no light from it
   exudings
none where we stand
   in nettles

clay of shoulder, groin
  of lost sea
    of face.

The red sun
  keeps on coughing.
A shiver
in the branches. Trees
  bowing to earth
swish, in an arc.

We wait on the dike.
The bulls wallow on
are sleepy. Catarrh smoke
surrounds the sun.

The light, again
  beaten out of kettles
strips the pewter river

the dike path trembles
green. A thistle
strikes a nerve. Creosote
and pitch. Palmer's bones.

Your eye absorbs light.
Wood doves quaver. An
owl, a linnet. The sun
expires. Warm
  with Palmer's creatures
the night comes on glorious
  pilgrim with
    divining rod
      walking stick.

FOUR:
Cool Zebras of Light

ON BEING RAVISHED BY AN ANGEL

He fell through stars
through polluted air
to reach you sleeping.

You've wanted him to come
have kissed David's
ivory balls and wound
the figurine in silk, in
rituals of craving.

You saw him
on an English street
in a German pub, smiling
near a yucca in the west.

When he wakes you, and
you turn over moist
warm, surprised, let him
kiss you, let him rub
his hot celestial cock
against your groin, let
him drive it in--as slick
as steel, ravishing

and when he explodes
and floods your navel
know, love, that he'll
withdraw more easily
than he came, leave you
to recall the sound
of his wings beating
out of the room away
from the castle, on
to other hungry dreamers.

Come into the next room.
I want to hold you.

HOW THE HORSE RUNS

1

Why don't you
come inside?
There's light here
and a
revolving eye.

2

It seems so easy
to write *zero,*
a downer. What
would Leander have
done swimming
believing
Hero would
receive him?

3

Plus and minus signs
cling like nettles to
fur. We rake them down
with a free hand, or
with a tied hand.

COOL ZEBRAS OF LIGHT

Your fists
are warm
against my ribs

The musk of love is
hot mercury
pressed between
layers of skin

At last
cool zebras of light
are feeding

IN THE WORLD: Hands

I know
what drifting means.
water, pellucid
gathers where friction
is applied, a
callous, rich and crusted
tough flakeskin,
delays a final
eruption.

Your hands
so soft between the
fingers
       touched
in the dark
and bitten.

Joined
our hands take shape
swell and blister.

You have to say
we are in lust
want to be had
blisters burned black
by weeds.

Draw your hand
over my face.
I'll wait.

TANGENTIAL RAIN

You stand sideways
in the light.   I love
your body, have, shall
and will.   I see everything
as a wedge.   Tell me.
There's meat in the
butcher shop window. . .
what's left?
Please, pass out of
my life, now, sideways,
just as you came.
Let it rain.

VIPERS OF THE MIND

My brain flashes
crystals of light,
no panic, no fright.
I have dug
someone's grave
with my teeth.
Still twitching
he lies beside me
on a beach.
I kiss him, bury him.
I do not even know
his name, or why he came.

NAIL IN THE SKULL: ENGLAND

Gargoyles strangle themselves
in red payphone meter boxes (they
look different in california)

or so I feel
    and you
owing more, I think, than
    health cards, sandpiles,
pounds, more than fractured plans

acclimatizing

and nerve to nerve
eye driven into the brain
nerve nerve
smash squash slush computer-juice
nerve, nerve, nerve

at that point
where the delta sinks under
its effluvium of crap
gin sniffings cliches
    (nothing chatters
        nothing is boring)

what we pretend to say, do say
we don't mean. the guise
of vigor, bravura,
metaphoric connections,
speech. venus in the univer-
sity quad behind her barricade.
apollo as a flower person,
the treatment--

where the stream spits clear
    not where the boats are
        or the boys fishing
or the beasts
                or the volcano,
here!

EACH HALTING CAR, EACH CARBURETOR

The hour crawls, a dismal
stretch of beginning & end

a carnelian jam. For five days
I heard you coming, not

believing you would refuse.
why don't you come? The cars

in the street are slow, they
drive on, choking. The

antique telephone is dead,
How to reach the fens

alone? I want peace
not despair, not light

slashing the retina, not the
dead lip nerve. Bullets

are here, so is the knocking
stroke of my heart. I

huddle in a corner, foetal
and want to die. Why don't

these messages get through?
there is glue in the mailbox

it will stay, until we are old
and can't see, can't recall

the shrill nerve of this night
twilight, fraught.

PARROTS

My mood tonight
howls blacks and reds.
I could fuck tables
chairs, dish
washers or owls.
The self won't do.
I observe my leg.
Nothing ascends.
My hand rests
by a cup, so
calm.   In my brain
parrots eat one another.

SLEEPWALKER

You are moving naked
in sleep, in your
warm bed, in your room
(you need socks,
a sweater, shoes).
You are coming
to like wearing
ripped things.

I walk in my sleep.
A bird drags over
my heart. I am cold.
In a few hours
it will be morning.
This day will flash
for you with a silver
light. Extend your
hand, waking, from
beneath your quilt.
Touch me.

LOVE POEM

A dead bird
this morning
in the back yard

A wren
by the chrysanthemum
its breast

chewed open. Cat
or skunk ravenous
for heart and lungs.

Feathers stir
in the wind. A
small tick (orange)
shivers and creeps
into the orifice,
into cold meat
and muscle.

I see you, love,
your brown eyes
open and still
lying on the green
surface of the moon
and I am eating
your heart.

HUBRIS

1

Each time, you say
you feel like a virgin:

each nerve swollen
with blood & bitten

is ravished afresh, the
ripped cloth wound

over your loins
lifts off, tightens

ensnares you symbolically,
against your will, loving it.

2

For me
each encounter is

a million hours old.   Perhaps
that's why I'm

anxious, don't
waste time pretending

we have just met in a
tropical garden, on

monastery land.   I want
to leap past gestures

we know, to savor cin-
namon, eat crushed thyme

and fall, locked, with you
through to that kingdom

of exhaustion, wet
breathing nerve-and-sinew
wisdom, burning the gods.

YOU HAVE MATTERED TO ME,
I HAVE MATTERED TO YOU

I want to go in
deeper than your teeth
deeper than your throat
into your brain
to find a space there
and mark it out
with rust and blood
a place with a bed
magnificent, and a
lust-rose chanting
splendid, ravished.

Now, when you cough, or cry
missing me (do you) does
your brain shake, as mine
shakes, crashing its love-
furniture over the floor
tinder against a prow?
tell me now:
has it been simple?
have you done it
with a knife?   can you
really cut me out of your life?

NIGHT REGRESSION POEM

I don't know
who you are
yet
you are
weakening me

I don't sleep
and once under
naked
you drift in
and poise on my
chest and blow
breath on my
hair

the door groans
letting you in
the clock
skips
and the furnace
rattles breaking
chains

I pretend
I'm a child
cradled
in sweat, I
want you to say
whether
you are innocent
I want to sleep
I want you to
take me.

ROLL OVER, LONGFELLOW

Was it wild
    and you found it, or
did you
    find it and were wild

there's no secret
    it was wild
and was female
    while I lift it

you are male and
    are my mover, if
my mouth bites
    then my sperm will

I won't be sorry
    that I've moved it
and I love you, if you
    find it

breasts and womb
    let me love you,
let me, let (her)
    be there

in an honor, to be driven
    as my shoulder, as my
groin is, towards your moving
    towards your tongue and

will it hurt you when I
    will you hurt me
as I hurt you as you
    lift me, will it hurt?

TRANSITION POEM

The moon delirious
swims through clouds.

You have learned to
sleep against me
my back against your chest.

This poem is easy.

I see that having
is flesh transformed

coming to touch--
skin to skin, bone
to bone, hair to hair.

Our loving has passed over
a volcano.

THERE IS THIS END FOR THE NIGHT

There is this end
for the night: it

will be there
pulverizing bones

beating water
into silt

or, it shall ride
like black dawn

meeting itself
east, over the sea.

We feel its breath
and, like it, draw closer

into a doubled
morning rose.

WEDNESDAY EVENING

Everyone, it seems,
complains.

But not now. How
can I keep on
trusting you?   you

bring me light--an
odor of plums, tin,
and silver cooling.

Who was at the door?
Don't be angry again.
Why should I leave the bath?

I know you have scattered
the brains of poems
over my pillow.

WHO CAN TASTE THE END OF HIS TONGUE

The tails of horses hang
as if no wind could stir them

a cloud attaches itself
to a pole

full of vitamins and gin
a good life follows us in

rain is coming some say,
others say snow

a cloud shreds into scraps
of silk, of exploding
white fish air sacs.

THE SEA

None of this is new:
each morning
my blood climbs
as if
for the last time.

SADISM POEM

Your bath lasts an hour
behind a locked door.
To use force won't work.
The carpet tacked to the
wall above your bed
sags lower.   Why is it
that every house we've
been in is eventually
reduced to screaming?
You thrust hatpins
through your cheeks
--just another high,
better than grass, bloodier
than acid.

SCISSORS

The scissors work
this time, for the last
time. You've said
you're not returning.
Something is rotten,
no intimacy or exchange
of breath, it seems,
can draw meat back
into health, fit to be
eaten. (I think of you
screwing in the baths
& being screwed). I
won't drop to the floor
for crumbs, or wail
that you have left me
burning for the word
that wouldn't come, to
resolve us finally,
for another week, month,
another year.

NIGHT FRIEND

You were finished with the night,
you said, and the sea.
Only steps of bone
leading home.   Burial site
for the viscera of deer.

You had lost heart,
you said, alone.
I knelt, proved that
beetles die, scream,
spit blood.   You
lit a fire, disrobed
and washed your body
in the sea.

A star
slid in the sky.   A boat
of travellers going
to a war sank in the waves.

Bury me, you said, desperate,
on a rack of poles and hide,
on a butte.   I cut
your throat.

ON FALLING FROM YOU

Cold stars
have said it all

and turbulence
dies, misfiring
meaning to kill

you. Still as a
naked archer frozen
in ice, through eons

of blizzards (what
new creatures will lap
up pools of fire). . .

that we were one and
one. Whatever is creased
to make a fan, whatever

craves to dance, and can,
as I fall from you, as
you leave, mountains of

ice rise, vast peaks
of blue and white, who
knows, how can I know?

those barking monsters
and craters are
the frozen tongues of god.

I thought that to fall
was to know, I thought
that to know was to fall.

FIVE:
Honey and Thorns

GAUGUIN'S CHAIR

1

The night is a lizard
beneath my shirt. The gas-
light is cold. The candle
I burn for you melts.
I would never whip a
woman, nor trip a beggar
crawling in spittle
in the street. I intend
to pay the rent. Most beds
are narrow. A tree of lemons
swung over ours. Branches
shook down black fat cherries.

2

I suck ribs and crack
kneejoints, find wine
and water in dream, fever,
hallucination. Polyps
cover my tongue.
An arrow rides
through my throat and lungs.
Come back! See how the night
burns flowers around the
door, trees in the window.

3

In the dark I said
"God is not living in the valley,
he is staying here with us."
You said, "God is a lily of the
valley, he is steel." That was
before the black house rat hung its
brother

from your easel, where I found it,
dying. See how you leave me.

4

When you came to Provence
I possessed one shoe, no
socks or soap, wore
no underwear. My tongue
ached for honey, a rope over a
rafter. I had smashed my clock,
had no books, painted
flowers and appletrees in blood
thinned with urine, thickened
with dung. Only sheep in the
orchard saw me, and gigantic
sunflowers waving hordes
of bees. I hate my lard
white skin! You almost drive me
to divert the world's vomit
back into its own throat.
You are halves of spiked iron
closing in on me.

5

I set the candle
on your chair, two books:
arms, back and seat
of chair. The candle
burns free of the tip.
Hot wire through knuckles
through cheek, tongue,
loin, hip and ankle.
My arms seem free, act.
The action cools my brain.
I can almost sing.

111

Outside, wheatfields swirl hair.
Seductive black birds--shock
patterns, brittle, raging, green.

I love you.   I love you.
And if I had killed you
as you were dying I would have
held you, would have lain
full-length upon you until
your feet were still.

MT. SAN GORGONIO ASCENT

(Mt. San Gorgonio, 13,400 ft., is the
highest peak in southern California)

1

We had come to a hill.
The path fell to a ravine.
Blue pine and fir.
Pellucid atmosphere.

Our speed set to the terrain.
Who should precede.
Talkers to the rear.
In the lead the walker

who would determine
the breaks, appraise
dangerous places, streams,
fallen trees, the shale.

Dung from the ranger's horse,
dust raked up by boyscouts,
Slushy Meadow, Dollar Lake,
the Saddle, grit along the way.

No gloom in our minds,
no beasts
under a canopy of sun,
no threat of storm.
Calm.

2

The sun burned down
swung its force
through the manzanita brush
burned ant trails bronze
burned ponderosas with its salt
seized the switchbacks for its own.

3

Then, on the trail
you described your *Play
for an Ancient Singer:*
the topic was John
the theme an old soprano--
a chasm gargling splendor
clad in an antique spasm.
That sodacracker voice
wound up to sing
a victrola spring.
The orchestra blatted.
The speed was overkeyed.
The throat was scratched.

4

I reached for sand.
A barbed tail with hot brown
skeletal divisions
snapped into an arc
to strike.
The scorpion struck
and missed.

5

At the next break
(you had not so far
spoken) your words counted.
Your question was a point:
"Who do you think I am?"
Your arc began
in the east, arabic,
saw Europe, New York,
whaling boats, Japan. . .
but who, Joe, baptized you?
Whom have you baptized?

The poet Clough,
lopped off in his prime,
wrote a limpid and stunning line:
"He is not far from home"
said Arthur from the water.

Water is distance.
Dollar Lake, icebright, lies
behind us.   Arthur
on his back strokes water
one hundred years ago.
No swimming here.
Nor is there runner's track.
It is all ascent.
One can, of course,
chin himself in a tree
if his hair is short.

6

And John?
We are hardly kin
are dimly brothers
have been creamed by
many saints and prophets
(including his)
of dubious sex:
we know the desert,
eat locust, snail
and ant, thistle plant,
cactus bits speared
on a two-tined fork.
We choke
swallowing goat's milk,
pluck icons from the sand,
search for the lost sheep,
retrieve only the tether.
We affix a halter, set
bridlebells to shake
force in the sexual bit
brave derelict weather. . .

John is in the well!

Tetrarch has put him in!
And coiling up from a stone
Herodias wants to free him!

7

Eyestalks averted.
Skin retracted, throbbing
head exhibited. Mucus
odorous as gas.
Nerve-ends red
over the head.

Blast a trumpet for Jokannon?

I can only watch
as a leech (fig-sized,
jugular blood) enraged
at the source's drying up
bursts.

8

At a drop below
hangs a cloud, mercurial.
The mountain it claims
floats green, lung-red, and blue.
Pines flare. Boulders
glow. Light falls.
Total mountain,
total drift of mist,
of flesh. The trance
is my own.

My hand is a peach
attached to a limb
swung over a gorge.
It hangs beyond all reach
gathers ripeness in.

Ichor swells the vein,
proceeds to the nipple end.
A bee strikes, hovers over.

9

I have forced mice into stockings
tied them
so that their toes
(rice beads) and a whisker
or two broke through.
I have held them under water
seen them wiggle,
struggle, plunge, seen
their blood run.

I fail to see! I am velvet
skin crevice
between the halves,
stem attached. . .

Find Jerome!
Where is John?
Those mendicants, medicine men!

Each of us has hallucinations
and will not be denied!

10

I reach a switchback, alone,
lose drift and accent.
Reins fall.

There is neighing.
I laugh.
The sound is brittle.
It turns to stone,
tumbles, falls as bone.

The flesh, wild, persists.
The ox shudders and drops.
The flesh, wild, persists.
The kid who has pissed her pants
cowers. The dancer crumples.

Better than we can
the scarab in the tomb
pierces doom; so does
the slavering dog
and the snout sniffing roots.

Something is latched in (gong)!
Something is added (cloak of hair)!
Something at the center (smoke)--
We can't leave flesh behind
unless we slaughter it.

11

We reach the summit.
The snow burns; we feel it.
Our feet
no longer beat but shuffle,
constricted by
snarewire drawn tight.
Our lungs crowd our throats,
our ears snap and burn.
Air
cuts over, through,
freezes sweat
on chest, loins
and back, smashes
the self.
We are mirrorless,
utterly.

THE DISCOVERY OF HONEY

(for Hans Combecher,
  Kerkrade, Holland)

your parents and sister,
dead in the war,
in a train departing from
Cologne strafed...

I *Prelude*

Mornings
our bodies assume
a special beauty:
warm hairs wet
with sleep, nipples &
phallus brought straight
by dreams, by visions
of those we lack, by
the excesses we crave--
the malodorous armpits
of an anchorite.

II *To Cologne Cathedral*

past rails and fences
past cement bridges
rivers and towns, trains
whirring past, elaborate
switches and signals
to Cologne Cathedral
late, seeing it again
in rain, black stone
perforated and hung
with gargoyles, finials,
steaming tympanum
of angels soot-winged
intent upon the feet
of Jesus.

yesterday, in Kerkrade,
you said that we
cooperate with God.
the white nuns understood:
to efface the self
is not necessarily to
erase it. saints
are nurtured here
or nowhere, the soul
tormented by mistakes,
the mind fractured, locates
a stream, winds past
razors, past boulders
in motion, to a semblance
of light.

III *The Burn goes on.*

and the burn goes on:
anxieties of the hour, the
victim's numb--in factories
schools, beds, bathrooms,
auditoriums.
              the delirious
wasp rolls over, the
hummingbird sucks nectar,
the lamb grabs the
ample tit of its mother.
wheat and barley raise
their grain, potatoes wither,
grapes fall onto sand, the
rose succumbs then blows.

IV *Before the Altar*

our candles are dim,
shadowed like our eyes,
their tallow torn from our
ribs. the baptismal font
swims in gasoline. we've

pasted bills due, bills paid,
letters frosted with obscenities.
to the font. we
burn bitter fat on altars
fashioned of beer cans
aspirin tins, brown
stickpins driven beneath
our nails and then withdrawn.

the organ shakes the pilasters.
incense drifts golden smoke
towards communion blood
and wafer. the priests
wear green, the acolytes
red and white. sacramental
gong. stone angels on
gothic porches protect stone
saints, smiling on them.

who kneels here? whose ear
blares that the specter,
man, wears the
refurbished grace of a
tarnished absolute, main-
tains an ecstasy derived from
licking his wounds?

to exist is to relish mud,
to taste formaldehyde, to
revile the dawn, to crush
pustules with the thumb, to
plant rare minerals in
ordure, and bite the wrenched
psyche, the pitchfork
thrust into the glands
of the suicide. let's murder
God in the cathedral!

See. we are in the rain
swallowing hail mixed with
prepackaged quantities of
shit! maimed trees drag
claws over the ground
towards our backs and heels.

how to crawl to you
thorn-wearer, thorns driven
in through the skull
blunt ends forming a
diadem? don't withdraw
your arm when we bite,
spread wings over us

as we move, move
expecting honey among
the thorns, splendid ichor
flooding the rocks; we should glow
more than be lost or
merely endurable! we did
not seek these straits!
we should be beautiful
in your sight.

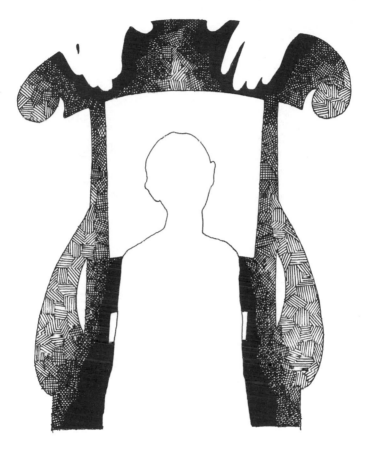

Interview

With Billy Collins—April, 1974

COLLINS: *Unlike most poets you didn't start writing poems until rather late in your life. What took you so long to get started?*

PETERS: Delays via academe, I guess. Ever since childhood, when I used to stand on the edge of my dad's gravel pit pretending I was Clark Gable, I wanted either to be an actor or a writer. I tried writing a novel in high school— a dreadful, sad thing about Lidice, the Czech town destroyed by the Nazis. I wrote it out on wallpaper books, and thought it a super work of art. Even in those days I guess I was sort of fancy—aesthetic you might say. So then the military and writing imitations of Gertrude Stein. And college, where I completed the whole stint from B.A. to Ph.D. in six calendar years, specialist in Victorian literature—dissertation on poetry and other arts in the 1890's.

I published a sourcebook, *Victorians on Literature and Art*, wrote and published a book on Swinburne's principles of art, spent eight years co-editing a three-volume edition of John Addington Symonds' letters—in other words, floundered, with a certain amount of energy, towards tenure, the professorship, good family and society things.

So, what took me so long to get started as a poet? The death of my young son Richard: that unlocked the poetry—a way of maintaining sanity in the face of this absurd, one-day illness and death: how to deal with it? nursery school in the morning...dead by suppertime. The only complaint a stomach ache. I was in bed with him all day reading Thomas Mann's *The Magic Mountain*. I've never finished the book. After this, the sort of safe, repressed life I'd been living made little sense. I kicked over, wrote poetry like mad and some novels, still unpublished, wrote a play produced by the Cubiculo Theatre in New York. And have made the transition into writing-poetry-times, amen.

COLLINS: *Did your son's death have any carry-over influence on your later poetry? I mean, do you find that that experience taught you to write in any way you still write?*

PETERS: Yes, because the death of my son tied in with my sense--strong then--of the self as victim in life. To step over towards this closure: victims suffer, and hence, poetry derives from suffering. Poetry becomes an anodyne for the absurd pointlessness of life. It took nearly ten years to resolve Richard's loss; and it took a turbulent session on the mattress of a therapy group to see that I had held onto that death as my clearly-given, heaven-derived sign that life is super-crud: my badge into the company of sufferers.

My loss was selfish, is what I'm saying. I didn't miss Richard as much as I luxuriated in my own victimization. Does that make any sense? It wasn't until I let go that I saw how absurd and whining I had become. Which is not to say that *Songs for a Son* whines. I feel that somehow those poems came out tougher, much less sentimental and, I hope, more cathartic and universal than my own psyche was.

Thereafter, my life lay about in colorful, wild chaos. To Europe with a guy I'd fallen in love with(it might as easily have been a girl) filling in a role as Verlaine, creating various torments as a part of the suffering indigenous to art. Perhaps there was a sense that I needed a *specialty*; my specialty would be guts, visceral, conglomerating pain, and stoic, majestic ascensions amidst the muck and ordure, a sort of mad Sophoclean vision larded over with a good stiff spread of Camus. Sure, put out thine eyes, do

125

it thyself, Oedipean...and let your rage clamor, your fists
strike blood, and then you may move towards a sort of
animal calm: be the beast waiting in the field, turned head
to other beasts, other horses, waiting for the next blows,
or for the stunning...or for temporary joy.

I don't reject this stage of my career; I'd like to go down
in poetry as the celebrator of man as victim, and beasts as
victims. There's energy there, and beauty there, as I hope
my butchering poems show.

COLLINS: *Do you find that your academic work had
any influence on the kind of poetry you ended up
writing?*

PETERS: Hard to say. Off the top of my head, my
academic background served in a couple of ways to
influence the kind of poetry I have written and write:
first, in a negative sense, I rebelled against academic
approaches to poetry. Now I know that these approaches
are as various as the sizes and shapes of women's breasts
and men's balls; but I had been trained on the New Critics
during the early fifties, and a poem was then a machine,
an intricately jewelled watch, full of images and inter-
connections to be explained with as much sense of myth,
intellectuality, and complexity as possible; also good
poems possessed an intricate verbiology which had little
directly to do with a poet's real feelings. I wanted my own
poems to be almost journalistic in their plainness, direct-
statement poems of such surface ease that any intelligent
somewhat trained reader would feel at home with them,
and only later discern hidden excellencies. In my own way
I wanted my surface-meaning poems to have the intricacies
of a Swiss watch...every part needed, all parts integral,
tight, swinging within their neat, little rat-cage interiors,
elevating the reader's sensibilities with sound and sense.
My poems to my son were meant to give the illusion that
a five year old child could understand them...note "the
illusion," for obviously I sprinkle words about that a
child would not understand. I wanted a rhythm so plain

that it would finely complement the simple diction. And all this was before I had read any amount of projective verse. In fact, Williams then to me was at best a couple of poems. "The Yachts" and something about burning a Christmas tree. Neither poem moved me very much. Williams was dull, I thought.

My rhythms for *Songs for a Son* I borrowed from a pop song high on the charts at the time: "Waterloo" as performed by Stonewall Jackson. The piece is still around and turns up occasionally on country-western stations. The number glues together around a driving Salvation Army bass drum rhythm. I played "Waterloo" loud, so loud that it hurt my ears, during a lot of the writing of *Songs for a Son*. It was a way of keeping sane...you know, pound on something, attack, as a way of externalizing and driving down your grief. This, combined with simple language, or the illusion of it, produced my own projective verse. You can imagine then what discovering Williams meant to me...a veritable opening of the waters. So, I've meandered from the question here: I think my ear has whatever subtlety it has because of my training in traditional poetry.

COLLINS: *Did your specializing in Victorian poetry have any influence on your style? What did you learn, for example, from Tennyson or Swinburne?*

PETERS: Victorian poetry has been important. Those splendid writers were considerably more than lace cuffs, bushy beards, assafoetida, and starch. Tennyson and Swinburne had two of the finest ears in all of English poetry. And *In Memoriam*, Tennyson's masterpiece, is an amazing gathering of lyric forms in the guise of an elegy. Of course, there are weak moments, and also a wild vibrant energy at times gone mad. One of the glories of Victorian poetry, in fact, is exuberance. I think T.S. Eliot complimented Tennyson on that somewhere. See, if your energy is vast, and your talent equal to it, your poems will be outpourings, like great rivers of sound and idea. You

can afford to oscillate between passages of a taut intelli-
gence and great creative skill and passages that serve as
resting places along the river, less demanding, lulling,
moments for regirding the creative loins, so to speak, for
the next turn. What the New Critics insisted on (borrow-
ing from Poe and Coleridge) was the standard of the poem
as an "energy construct," a neat machine to be absorbed
at one sitting. Poe said that a poem was no good unless it
could be so absorbed. This, as you know, meant the death
of the long poem! And also the death of a poem containing
rises and falls of intensity.

There was something dumb and frenetic and constipated
about most poetry of the 1940's, as though a knife-
wielding monster waited to chop off fingers, balls, breasts,
if you wrote poems that couldn't be read comfortably in a
single sitting. I exaggerate, obviously. I'd like to recapture
something of the qualities the Victorians had but which
we've lost. I want to sense the range of a poet's abilities—
excesses and deficiencies—within a single poem. Is that
asking too much?

COLLINS: *No, that sounds desirable. Williams seems to
get into some of that long-poem peaking and valleying in
"Paterson" but then it's often by default or by deferring
to the documents he mixes into the poem; at those points
the linear run of the poem is almost suspended. Let me
ask you this. Do you think that familiarity with the
history of English poetry is essential to a poet writing
today? In other words, should a poet know the limits to
which his predecessors have pushed the language so he can
push it farther?*

PETERS: How can you really know what you're up to as
a poet if you don't know what's preceded you? How
stupid you'd be if you thought you'd invented the elegy
by lamenting the death of a friend and tossing in a few
references to Nature, say a woodland motif from northern
Wisconsin or southern California, tossed on a few local
flowers, had a river tumble and mourn.

If you have little sense of the splendid achievements of

earlier poets, you'll only have a fumbling sense of what your own achievement should be; you won't know how high up to shaft the arrow. In other words, I do believe that your own poems will be better, and you'll be less content with dabbling if you are aware of what other poets have achieved.

It's a matter of knowing the bro-sisterhood you're part of. I see my own students contemptuous of earlier poets. They see little value in reading them, I'm afraid. Their brains would be more agile, astute, fertile, I believe, if they immersed themselves in older poets. Trained heads, yes. Better John Donne than James Tate; better Alfred Lord Tennyson or Algernon Charles Swinburne than W.S. Merwin or Galway Kinnell.

COLLINS: *Who do you write for? your friends, yourself, a fantasy of an outside audience at large?*

PETERS: I could say I write for myself, which I guess is what most writers are supposed to say: a removal of self from caring about an audience. Poetry doesn't attract wide audiences; of course, Ginsberg is the exception, and Rod McKuen. Poetry is an extension of the poet's private life. The poet is himself an exclusive act! The poet behaves exclusively!

There's some truth here, of course. I began writing out of a need to deal with my own grief. And I put the poems away for three years, showing them to no one, before I took them out, then wrote more, and put them away for three more years. So, a total of six years passed before I tested them on magazines. When did my sense of being a professional happen? I suppose when I published the first of these poems in *The Fiddlehead*. It seemed possible that the poems might move in the world, touch lives, invite contacts and letters from persons liking them. My guess is that most poets, whether they admit it or not, want a public. If not, why the scrambling to get noticed by *The American Poetry Review* and other showcases, to get on CCLM committees, to get readings at prestigious places, to get books nominated for awards, all that. Yes, to be

honest, I want as wide and various a public as I can reach.
I want my poems to touch lives, particularly the lives of
the young, and I want to know that I have touched them.
Perhaps that's why I do as much public reading of my
work as I do. I've assumed that since I started writing
professionally at age 39 I sense the good things out there—
the rewarding people, the fame—and I want to experience
them, all of them while I'm still alive. I've never thought
much about posthumous fame. Being a poet is fun, in
addition to the discipline and hard work involved. Why
not enjoy the fun, why not know too when you have
changed some beautiful reader's perspective on life, art,
caring. To reach a reader, this was, is, for me an act of
love. I need acts of love.

COLLINS: *To get back to your first book of poems,
"Songs for a Son." You mentioned that this was a set of
elegiac responses to the death of your son. Did you find it
difficult to work with such an emotionally loaded subject
matter?*

PETERS: No. I seem to write best from an emotionally
loaded situation. Or, rather, let me say that for the first
years of my poetry-writing life that was true. A couple of
years ago I started experimenting with what I call "parable
poems." Sort of surreal things, in which I generally took
from my dream or from day-hallucinations whatever trans-
pired in my scrim-head-brain. I wrote these up inventing
funky rhymes and rhythms. These generally, when they
work, have an objectivity very different from the self-
tormented, celebratory manner of my first two books.
The Red Hill Press, incidentally, brought these out as
Holy Cow: Parable Poems. But I do think that my typical
poem, if poets have typical poems, derives from an
emotionally loaded situation. I hunger to write that
perfect non-pain, non-fucked up, non-undergoing poem of
celebration, a love poem, so positive, complex, dedicated
in its life. I envy poets who can write such poems. I want
to be more than a latter-day Camus. And that's why my

recent work, a series of poems on Ann Lee (published by Liveright), the incredible woman who founded the Shakers in the late 18th century, is an ambitious attempt to move into the psyche of a stranger. And yet, surprisingly, her psyche, as I sense it and render it, is much like my own in my early books. I guess you do what you do. It's that simple. And my newest book, *Picnic in the Snow,* a verse treatment of the life of Ludwig of Bavaria, is a similar large attempt to move out of myself.

COLLINS: *You said earlier that poetry was a way of keeping sane. How do you mean that?*

PETERS: I meant that the act of writing, occupying various hours of one's waking life, can focus energy away from pain and tragedy and can divert that energy into organized rhythms, patterns, systems. The sense of creating is then positive, a celebration of life-forces, and keeps one moving to rhythms of sanity.

COLLINS: *Someone once called you an "entrailist" because your poems are so full of strong anatomical images: liver, scrotum, ribs, gizzard, this sort of thing. How come? Is there a pattern here?*

PETERS: Yes, there's a pattern. It goes something like this: joys and threats pile up against us and for us. Things that happen to our external physical selves, like cuts, bruises, we can treat. But there is an interior threat as well, lots of them: organs going sour, turning to mash-mush. My dad had his stomach removed because of cancer. A grandmother died of gangrene from a ruptured stomach. My grandfather died of infection after being gored by a bull. My own son complained of no powerful symptoms the day he died. In other words, you often can't tell when your own body internally betrays you until it is too late. And being an *entrailist* is for me a way of allaying my own fears of being this sort of victim. Life is a matter of confronting guts, of taking care of our own, of realizing their vulnerability, of knowing how easily they are abused.

131

When such poems work, they hopefully resolve their ugly painful subject matter as works of art and beauty.

COLLINS: *Often you place uncommon words up against simple ones, words like ichor, tympanum, perineum, arbutus; is this for the sake of precision, sound?*

PETERS: My image of Roethke, whom I vastly admire, is that he had a special gift of dropping in an unusual word when you were not expecting it, words that most of us would need the dictionary for. And I love that in him. Yeats did that well too. I love language, playing with it, the possibilities of words are so immense. An ideal poem would hide words like those you mention in a pure Dick-and-Jane style. Exaggeration? Only partly. And why isn't every word in the language possible for the poet? What I object to is word decoration, Shakespearian groanings and strainings to get lots of polysyllabic words plus a formal tone full of inverted verse-sentence structures...you know what I'm talking about. A word like *tympanum* (I hear Yeats' "Byzantium" here) is delicious. It is actually a simple word in the way that its syllables interact, and the neat "ym"— "um" rounding off! You can do rich things with words like this. Of course, you can overuse them. I had favorite words I've vowed never to use again in poems; one is *raw*. And that's not a fancy word at all. Then again, I'd hate to use *perineum* in every third poem.

COLLINS: *What got you interested in the Shakers?*

PETERS: Complete serendipity. I took a wrong road, trying to find Saratoga Springs, New York, last summer and ended up at a Shaker Museum in Old Chatham. I bought a history of the sect at the museum. It struck me that this was a superb subject for a lengthy treatment, something I had hoped to find. I was tired of writing isolated poems, connected by threads to my own psyche, but nevertheless various. So I got to work within a week afterward and wrote frenziedly, almost possessed, completing a hundred poems in three weeks. I've been reworking and revising ever since. Ann Lee became a tremendous presence. I visited her grave near Albany weekly, as an energy source. Nothing mystical or sentimental. The grave was a fact of where whatever remains of her remains.

COLLINS: *Did this project move you in a new stylistic direction?*

PETERS: Actually, I move with forms I've used in the past, the narrative poem, the lyric. A number of these poems are songs, simple hymns. One, in fact, is written in a strange tongue. Others are monologues spoken by Ann as she deals with various crises in her life: the death of four children in infancy, imprisonment in a madhouse, dungeon cell, madness, sexual guilt, a turbulent crossing to America with her eight followers. So, the answer about the stylistic direction: more of the same, but, hopefully, better.

I felt encompassed by the Ann Lee sequence, as though there was no form inappropriate to it, A-B-C sequence, in the Kate Greenaway manner. Tremendous fun to write. Other poems incorporate Shaker hymns and Bible passages. Others give the illusion of very tight conventional forms. Ann Lee was a major visionary. I sincerely hope that my poems do her justice. She was a sort of female William Blake who diverted her visions into the creation of a religion. Yes, and historically, she was the female Christ!

COLLINS: *Prosody seems important to you; how do you find the right rhythm?*

PETERS: Oh, various things help. I know very little about formal prosody, actually, despite the fact that my book on Swinburne is on this topic and related esthetical matters, and that I served at one time as a trustee for the American Society of Aesthetics. I've always felt that if you trained your ear right, you didn't need to make a scientific study of prosody...you'd hear all you need to. This may be a limitation. Other poets really get into it and write all sorts of traditional prosodic forms as part of their discipline.

I've never gone that way. Rhythms dictate themselves to me. I hear the voice in the poem, one of joy, anguish, tension, questing, hurting or whatever, and play on a basic rhythm, almost metronomic in its base. Then I set about enriching that basic line with variations, and with slant-rhymes, vowel-music and the like. Understand, that what I describe seems to work for *me*.

COLLINS: *Auden said that poets submit their works in progress to an "internal Censor." Are you aware of having one? What's he like?*

PETERS: I like Auden's idea. I think mine operates best once a first draft is finished. These first are more like outpourings; I suspend my critical sense until I feel something like a first draft is done. Then I go to work, usually soon after the first draft, pulling, pushing, chipping, filing. Mostly deleting. I hardly ever write less than I need, usually more. I've seldom been able to flesh out a poem if there wasn't sufficient meat in the first place. I wonder if skinny poets work the same; is it harder to excise flab if you're skinny? It all comes down to what you want most: either to lose or to gain. Towards a new esthetic of creative acts!

The idea of censor obviously suggests that there are some subjects you won't touch with your poems. A tiny inner voice of conscience, or whatever, tells you when too much is too much. I'm inclined to be stubborn, and when a still small voice urges me not to write something, I generally go ahead and write it. The voice is useful primarily for telling me when an emotion is rendered excessively, and for what I call the *tact* required in revisions.

COLLINS: *How much of your imagery comes from your childhood?*

PETERS: I'd say a lot. Nature, farm animals, poverty, simplicity of language and form. I grew up during the thirties on a scrub-sand farm of forty acres in nothern Wisconsin. My dad scrounged for a living, WPA on a road crew for $40 a month, mechanic, farmer. We kept a cow, a pig or two, some chickens. Raised potatoes, corn, vegetables. Picked blueberries, raspberries, juneberries which Mother canned. My dad built our small house out of logs and tar-paper. The inside walls were covered with pieces of cardboard smashed flat. In the winter, northern Wisconsin is wretchedly cold; nipples of frost collected around the nail heads, and when the woodstove fires warmed things up, frost melted and dripped down in our faces as we lay in bed.

I romanticize that life now, but then I knew that there must be something better out there in the big wide world. My dad was nearly illiterate, but had a keen sense of language—natural metaphors, similes. And he taught himself to play six musical instruments. We had a band that played taverns when I was in high school. My mother washed clothes in an outdoor wash-house, without heat. We had no plumbing or running water, and until I was nearly through high school I did all of my studying by a single-wick kerosene lamp. There was a lake a half mile behind our house. I worked hard in the small fields. I loved the woods and spent a lot of time there, and in swamps and highland areas.

COLLINS: *Do you usually know exactly where you are going when you start a poem, or does the writing as you go along decide that for you?*

PETERS: The writing as I go along usually decides that. I almost never plan a poem out in advance. Some image or word drifts into my head. I put it down (the word) and proceed from there. Often I don't get past those two lines. Once in a while I depend for stimulation on other poets' poems. I open a book, my eye lands on an image, the image sets an image of my own going, and I'm underway. I've most consciously imitated Creeley's, Spicer's, Neruda's and Merwin's rhythms. Although Merwin's grand abstractions turn me off, his ear doesn't. I keep saying *ear* when I talk about poets. I may be perhaps too attuned to sound. I luxuriate in splendid sounds in poems, my own as well as other people's.

Bibliography

BOOKS OF POEMS

The Little Square Review No. 2: Fourteen Poems by Robert Peters, Santa Barbara, 1967.

Songs for a Son, W. W. Norton, Inc., 1967.

The Sow's Head and Other Poems, Wayne State University Press, 1968.

Eighteen Poems, privately printed, 1971, 1972, 1973, Irvine, California.

Byron Exhumed: A Verse Suite, Windless Orchard Chapbook No. 9, Purdue University, 1973.

Red Midnight Moon, Empty Elevator Shaft Press, 1973.

Connections: In the English Lake District, Anvil Press, 1972.

Holy Cow: Parable Poems, Red Hill Press, 1974.

Cool Zebras of Light, Christopher's Books, 1974.

Bronchial Tangle, Heart System, Granite Books, 1975.

The Gift to be Simple: A Garland for Ann Lee, Liveright/Norton, 1975.

The Poet as Ice-Skater, Manroot Books, 1976.

The Collected Poems of Amnesia Glasscock (*by John Steinbeck*) with a response by Robert Peters, Manroot Books, 1976.

Hawthorne, Red Hill Press, forthcoming, *with drawings by Carol Yeh.*

A Shaker ABC, Christopher's Books, forthcoming.

The Drowned Man to the Fish, New Rivers Press, forthcoming, *with drawings by Meredith Peters.*

LITERARY CRITICISM

The Crowns of Apollo: Swinburne's Principles of
Literature and Art, Wayne State University Press,
1965.

The Great American Poetry Bake-Off, essays on
contemporary poets, Margins Books, forthcoming.

EDITIONS

A Splendid Will: From the Writings of The Rev. Walter
B. Pederson, Bloomfield Hills, Michigan, 1960.

America: The Diary of a Visit, Winter 1884-1885, by
Edmund Gosse, ed. with David G. Halliburton,
Purdue University, 1966.

Victorians on Literature and Art: A Sourcebook,
Appleton Century Crofts/Prentice Hall, 1961.

The Letters of John Addington Symonds, 3 vols., ed.
with Herbert G. Schueller, Wayne State Univer-
sity Press, 1967, 1968, 1969.

Pioneers of Modern Poetry, with George Hitchcock,
Kayak Press, 1967.

Gabriel: A Poem by John Addington Symonds, with
Timothy d'arch Smith; Michael de Hartington,
1974.

A SELECTION OF CRITICAL ESSAYS

"Whistler and the Poets of the 1890's," in Modern
Language Quarterly, vol. 18, 1975.

"Toward an 'Un-Definition' of Decadent as Applied
to British Literature of the Nineteenth Century,"
The Journal of Aesthetics and Art Criticism,
vol. 18, 1959.

"Athens and Troy: Notes on John Addington
Symonds' Aestheticism," English Literature
in Transition, vol. 5, 1962.

"Swinburne's Idea of Form," *Criticism,* vol. 5, 1963.

"Verbal Musculature and Concealed Kinetics in the Early Poetry of Walt Whitman: A Study in Projective or Open Field Composition," *Kayak 8,* 1966.

"Funky Poetry: Allen Ginsberg's 'The Fall of America,' " *New* 22 and 23, 1973-74.

"Poetry-Biz or APR is Shot from Guns," *Margins* 8, 1973.

"The Poet as Pusher," *Margins* 13, 1974.

"The Poem as Spirit-Meat, or Michael McClure's Corpus of Poems are Delecti," *New* 24, 1974.

"The House that Jack Built has an Atwater Kent in the Living Room, or, Jack Spicer's Romanticism Didn't Come Easy," *Manroot* 10, 1974-75.

"Gab Poetry: The Art of Charles Bukowski," *Margins* 16, 1975.

"On Climbing the Matterhorn (Monadnock): Galway Kinnell," *Northeast Rising Sun,* vol. 1, 1976.

"Angels with genitals: with "The Female Gate" by Clayton Eshleman," on Clayton Eshleman's Coils, in *Margins* 9-11, 1976.

"The Great American Poetry Bake-Off, or, How W. S. Merwin Wins all those Prizes," *Manroot 11,* 1976.

Robert Peters teaches at the University
of California, Irvine, specializing in Victorian
literature and contemporary poetry. He has
published some fourteen books of poems
over the past ten years.